HIGH COUNTRY Poems

HIGH COUNTRY Poems

Inez Hunt

Filter Press, LLC
Palmer Lake, CO

Copyright © 2008 Frances Hunt Kiester. All rights reserved.

Library of Congress Control Number: 2008929401

ISBN: 978-0-86541-083-1

Published by
Filter Press, LLC
Palmer Lake, Colorado
www.filterpressbooks.com 888.570.2663

Cover Art by Jennifer Hancey
www.HanceyDesign.com

No part of this publication may be reproduced or transmitted in any form or by any means, electronic or mechanical, including photocopy, recording, or any information storage and retrieval system, without permission in writing from the publisher.

Printed in Canada

Dedication

For Sally Ann

My copper-haired grandmother
Who left me stories for a heritage.

Who knew all about homesteading
With four children growing tall,
And when to use the rod and when to spare
And how to make a poultice out of bread—
And how to spread a spider web on a fresh cut—
Who felt the sting of camphor could cure everything,
And recommended hot tea, even for a broken heart.

Who could remember
How it was when Quantrill took the cow
And shot the boy—
Who kept a pair of white lace stockings,
Bought in Vicksburg when the siege was on,
Folded in her bible with a rose.

Who taught me mysteries of maples
Blowing silver in the wind—

Who died at ninety six, still peppery—
Copper-haired up to the last—
A little tarnished and a little tired—
A little tired of "all this fiddle!"

Introduction viii

The Poems

High Country 1
How to Recognize a Young Poet 2
Poets Inarticulate 3
Ghost Writer 4
Ghost Town House 5
Thin Skin, the Red-Haired Kind 6
Moment Unaware..7
Lake City Church 8
Old House at Rosita 9
Story of Ruby 10
The Ghosts of Cripple Creek....................11
Story at Buckskin Joe Cemetery................12
Hessie 13
For Deer 14
Mountain Cemetery 15
Prairie Burial 16
Board Walk 17
Sand Creek at Chivington 18
New England Church
     in a Mountain Town 19
Vista, Too Wide...20
"Don't Go to Gothic" 21
Curtain Call 22

The Silver Ghost of Fryer Hill 25
Stone Cutter 26
Of Burros and Men 27
Ruin at Romely 28
Rough Etching 29
School House, Abandoned 30
Ellie Mae 31
At Redstone 35
Chipeta at Montrose 36
The Galloping Goose at Old Telluride 37
Keepers of the Sheep 39
Scarlet Thread 41
Loss 42
Old Construction Worker
    at the Circle Bar 43
Ticket to Silverton 45
Ranch Story 46
Why I Stay 48

Introduction

Mary Jane Massey Rust
Colorado Springs, Colorado

Inez Hunt was a historian, short story writer, and nonfiction author, but the heart and mind of this extraordinary woman was in her poetry. Her first book of poetry, *Windows through the Wall*, was published in 1956. *Ghost Trails to Ghost Towns* followed in 1958 and featured photographs by Inez's dear friend Wanetta Draper. Then came *High Country Ghost Town Poems* in 1962. The special friendship of the two women led to years of collaboration, not to mention fun and exciting adventures.

Though poetry may have been her first love, Inez managed to write books that focused on local history as well. *Black Pioneers* traced the history of the Bass Family, whose presence in the Pikes Peak area began when they came to the region with Colorado Springs founder William J. Palmer. *Lightning in His Hand: The Life Story of Nikola Tesla* remains a much-sought-after biography, now in the rare book category.

Inez and her husband, Nelson, lived for a time in the historic Colorado Midland Depot in Manitou Springs, which had been remodeled into a private home. Nelson, who sported a real, full, white beard, was the favorite Santa Claus at the local North Pole attraction in Cascade, Colorado. Together, the Hunts left an indelible mark on the Pikes Peak region.

Inez wrote hundreds of published poems and fortunately left a treasure of unpublished works to her daughter, Frances Hunt Kiester. Inez's poetry will resonate with those fortunate to live in the American West, and especially with those who live in the Pikes Peak area. Her poetry includes a wide range of subject matter, from short comic verses to poignant reflections of ranch life and sometimes tragic stories of early gold miners down on their luck.

Inez's own words in the Foreword to *High Country Ghost Town Poems* (1962) convey that of all her writing, poetry was how she wanted to present the world that she saw.

> *These verses sketch the profiles I have seen in the high country. Some are of peaks—some of people and even the creatures which make up the western scene. Sometimes they are strong-boned profiles, clear and articulate—and sometimes fragmentary outlines caught faintly in the alpine glow.*
>
> *I seldom carry a camera as I go. I have known photographers who could catch the elusive, but I am usually grieved to find my camera did not record all I saw. Dim figures that are so clear to me disappear at the click of a shutter. Nor do I find any equipment that can record the voices I hear in these places.*
>
> *So I choose verse to hold the scene and to tell the story. If I have used first person to record so many stories, not mine, please forgive and remember— they told it to me that way.* —IH

High Country

This is high country,
Frigid and wounding sharp and raw
And more than match for any man
Who dares to stay.

I have heard her winter mutterings
And have seen old timers
Cast knowing glances as they said,
"It's the Sisters coming down to close the pass."
Then I have watched white Furies with their vengeful hands
Spill avalanche and death.

But I have seen this high country
Thaw and yield and flow
And murmur past a fern
And hide a fawn.

How to Recognize a Young Poet

Poets are born half human and half elf,
With pointed ears to catch the call of flying geese,
With hair that will not stay in place.
(We call them cowlicks, but that is not so)
They swirl to cover miniature horns…
But horns.

Eyes are important. They will be wide set
And large enough to hold
All the sun and tears it takes to make a rainbow.

Watch how they walk
With feet that sometimes do not touch the ground,
And often take them breast-high into the storm.

Their song may vary from as deep as heart
To heights where phantom fingers of a Debussy
Caress the shimmered scales.

There will be times when cloven hoof asserts itself
And forked tail wounds you if you come too close.
There will be wings that fold back out of sight
And always heart too big to hold.

You cannot capture them
And you must follow them afar
For they must walk alone.

Poets, Inarticulate

All poets do not write.
There is the flier with his jet who cuts the blue
That hangs between the earth and pale infinity...
The skier with his winter song of grace and flashing speed.
And there are homely things...a mother's hands
    at night...
The man who hoes straight rhythmic growing rows
To gamble with the sun and dust and rain.
And there is one who brings a moss rose for a memory,
And every soul who gropes by faltering candle of
    his dream
To translate God.

Ghost Writer

I know I shall never lie still.
Here on this earth it was so hard to sleep.
I shall never be content with everlasting rest,
Or six short feet of nothingness.
I am sure that I shall walk
At twilight, midnight, or whenever they let us go.
I shall walk on tiptoe
And peer over the shoulders of poets
Who get up because they cannot sleep
And write down words that flow like rills
Into their sleepless consciousness.
I shall slip words into their mouths
And push their pens
And whisper in their ears
And they will say,
"It just came to me in the night
And I wrote it down!"
And I will remember
And smile
And lie down again.

Ghost Town House

How does a house die?
First, someone shuts a door.

Then storms strike hard
To shake the chinking loose
And cold settles in a down-draft
Through a sodden flue.
Glass shatters or is stolen,
Leaving hungry holes.

The floors break through
Where memory grows too heavy for the joist.
The rats gnaw tediously along with Time
In little bites.

So, a home dies,
But death begins the day
The one who loves it
Locks a door and walks away.

Thin Skin, The Red-Haired Kind
A Story from Clear Creek

They said she was pretty once,
When Grandpa brought her here,
But I never saw her that way.

As I recall,
Her hair, once copper, wore a tarnished hue
Her skin, brown splotched and wrinkled.
Thin skin, the red-haired type,
Won't stand the mountain sun and freeze
And buffet of the dust-grimed wind.

They said she raised her family by herself
With Grandpa up and gone with each Chinook
To strike a high-grade vein or chase a painted face,
But back again late fall
To warm his feet
And eat dried-apple pie
And see the baby born a month ago.

They said Grandma was pretty once
But mountain sun and freeze and dust-grimed wind
All take their toll—
Especially of thin skin,
The red-haired kind.

Moment Unaware

He was an ornery one
And didn't half deserve his turn of luck,
But Fortune is a whoring jade
Who doesn't care
Whose lap she falls into
Nor where her kisses go
Nor who lets down her hair.

So Fortune filled his cup
As often as he drank it dry,
Until it dripped off both the points of his mustache
And wet his gaping shirt
That stretched across his barreled chest.

And so he drowsed
And became numb to either joy or pain
And never was aware of the exact moment
Fortune left him—
Nor even cared.

Lake City Church

There is a white church
With a child-like simplicity
And ghosts that haunt this place
Are those of little children
Sacrificed to build the west.

This was a man's country.
You seldom think of children
Except in cemeteries
Where the stones
Tell how the epidemic
Took its toll.

Here in the clean swept aisle
I see little girls
In starched white dresses
Walk to light an inner fire.

Outside, I think of small boys,
Reluctant to go in,
Who turn bright leaves in grubby hands
To wonder, "What is gold?"

In child-like churches such as these,
The words, "Except ye become—"
Keep crowding back
And I shed sophistication
In the snow-washed wind
And watch the fall turn cottonwoods
To altar fires.

Old House at Rosita

I couldn't tell you why—you'd think me daft,
Explaining why I bought this sagging place,
As useless as a long abandoned shaft
And scarred and lined as deeply as my face.
I can't explain why I can't tear it down
Nor make museum for the curious eye.
I only know it's best the old ghost town
Should slowly gray and with its day should die.
The hall stairway is rotted, soon to fall,
But there's no longer call to go up there,
Remembering wild roses on the wall
As pink as those she wore in her black hair.

I'd rather let it go—be past and done,
An old horse, loved and pastured in the sun.

Story at Ruby

She wasn't mountain born.
I brought her here
And folks said she would never fit this place
All rock and rough and hard,
And she, no bigger than a bar of soap after a big wash.

She didn't take to storing things
Or canning like a mountain woman should
With summers short.
But rather, when the air turned soft,
She danced tip-toe and braided calico into her hair
And later, gathered berries, eating as she picked
Insisting they were better warm with sun
And saying, "Why hoard sweetness like the bees
Who work all summer to be robbed!"

She wasn't strong enough
To fight hill storms.
She couldn't face the cold
And never lived to hush the baby in her arms.

Folks said she didn't fit into these hills,
But I remember that she fit the hollow of my arm.

The Ghosts of Cripple Creek

The ghosts of Cripple Creek walk quietly
And unobserved, save where our knowing eyes remember—
Save where we recognize the restless shadow forms.

Walk along Bennett with its tilting walks
And ghoul-eyed windows.
Feel the forms push you as they crowd forsaken streets
To walk their restless pace—a pace born of a fever
That cannot be quenched by death.

Loiter at Sixth and see if you can outline Womack
As he throws away his money to the crowd—
Ill-fated Bob, forgotten and as lonely
As the wind that cuts him through.

Watch the hawk soar upon the hill
Where a white horse rides straight into fog.
Watch Stratton dream before the Palace fire,
No longer puzzled by the weight of gold.

The ghosts walk quietly in Cripple Creek
And unobserved, except where knowing eyes
Remember and re-live.

Story at Buckskin Joe Cemetery

I came out west with him to see that he ate right,
Vegetables and bread and not just meat.
I kept his blankets clean
And put a hot iron to his feet on winter nights.

I kept his house
And saw he stayed home nights,
And I reminded him about his chores.
A man has to be told.

And when he died,
I starched and ironed his boiled shirt
And folded both his hands.
The preacher said he was a model man
And I knew I had done everything I could.
Then when I buried him,
I put a granite stone over his head
And then I put a fence around his grave.

Hessie

"Why did they name the town for the Postmaster's wife,"
I asked, "instead of him?"

The old timer shook his head,
And wrinkled his brow and filled his pipe.
"Near as I can recall," he drawled, "he was an outdoor man.
He wasn't much for detail and the like
And little pigeonholes confused him
And he never could remember
Whether the name was above or below.
It didn't matter.
Hessie always did them over anyway.

"Besides, someone had to mind the store
And she could boil the beans and heat the irons
On the big stove with the same wood
And watch the baby and talk to customers
While he went out to fish and pan a little on the side.
He could have struck it rich, you know.
Uncle Sam always sent the check made out to him
But folks just got the habit of saying,
'Send my mail to Hessie.' That may be how it was."

For Deer

The kindest thing you can do for deer
Is to throw a stone and teach them fear.
It wasn't fair. We coaxed with salt.
We fed the fawn. That was our fault.
Now blood lies red upon the ground
Where sanctuary once was found.
The kindest thing you can do for deer
Is to throw a stone and teach them fear.

Mountain Cemetery

Walk softly here
Where once they tenderly laid down their dead
So far from home.

Walk quietly
And breathe a prayer for peace
For all who sleep in these blue hills.
Straighten the graying picket fence
That stock have pushed in search of greening grass.
Fill up the hole the curious coyotes dug.

Brush back a tear
For one wild fragile rose
That climbs a stone where mother and a babe
No longer look upon a sunlit world
Save through the blue eyed flax.

Bow with your heart
To all the ghosts of men who lived by code,
Compelled to play each card exactly as it fell—
The unafraid—the strong—the uninsured.
Who died bequeathing to us all
Dim trails that lead forever to a western sun.

Prairie Burial

Why he had asked to be buried here,
I could not see—here in this pitiful array
Of tilted stones and markers, and
These thirsty junipers that fought a dusty hill
For root and life.

Down the warm slope, a rattler
Left a finger trail to slide beneath a rock
And sing a requiem.

A thunder mutter threatened to transform
An adobe road to no-bottom grease
Within an hour.

But why he chose this place,
I could not see,
Until I said, "I hate to leave him here alone,"
And one brown rancher said,
"He's not alone, Ma'am.
Why, my baby's right across from him
And Mom and Dad almost beside him,
Though you can't tell with the fence torn down.
Yesterday, we dug it here especially,— "
"You mean you dug it here—yourself?"
"We wouldn't let a stranger, Ma'am," he said.

Board Walk

Old walks run strange,
Worn smooth by vanished feet
And tilted as they settle into Time's quicksand.

In Central, once, they laid bright silver bricks
To be a sidewalk for the President.
Now silver bricks and presidents are gone.
One old board walk remains
To breathe a muffled chant
To all who pass this way.

Sometimes, when I walk on quiet days,
I hear the rustle of bright petticoats
That once caressed these boards.
Sometimes it is the silken step of barefoot child
Who strums a picket fence with broken stick
And drops crumbs of warm bread and sugar as he goes.

And sometimes I step aside
To let hobnailed and hurried boots
Go striding by.

Note: In 1873 President Ulysses S. Grant came to Central City on his tour through the West. To impress the president, mine owners laid ingots of solid silver to make a path to the Teller House Hotel so President Grant wouldn't have to dirty his boots when he stepped from his carriage.

Sand Creek at Chivington

The Sand Creek sun shines warm to heal
A wound that will not be healed.
The quicksand waits to avenge.
There is a chill under the cottonwood.

Green lizards mark their fine stitched trails
Into the shade of a sprawling gourd vine,
Seeded in Time and a red man's tragedy.

The curve of the creek is a hungry arm
Outstretched in remembering.
The morning deer has printed its track
Beside a broken arrowhead.

Far off, a wandering wind gathers the sand
Into yellow puff-whirls—
Spirits of old Indian fires
Still smouldering, still smouldering.

Note: Chivington, Colorado, was founded north of Lamar in the late 1800s and was a ghost town by the early 1900s. It was named for Colonel John Chivington, who commanded the militia at the Sand Creek Massacre on November 29, 1864. The attack destroyed a village of Cheyenne and Arapaho encamped near the creek. An estimated 150 to 200 Indian women, children, and elderly men were killed.

New England Church in a Mountain Town

Somehow, when you go west,
You can go western
In almost everything but God.

Oh, after a while, you get to thinkin'
Maybe God loves this new country after all,
Raw and big and terrible at times.
Maybe He even likes to walk under tall pines
In the cool of the day.

But women want a church, white—
Like the one back home.
So you humor them
The way you do when you put the curlicues
On the gables and the porch
And when you put the pump close to the back door.

After all, it's the women-folk
Who do most of the thinkin'
About the marryin'
And the buryin',
Maybe they don't want God homesick
For a house he knew.

Vista, Too Wide

High on the hill
They buried him beside the stony road
That looked across the valley to the town,
Where mines, the dance hall
And the tortuous daily trail
Had pressed for toll.

Someone remembered
To put flowers in a mason jar,
Now dirty and half full of leaves
And someone fearful
Of a vista, far too wide
Placed pickets like brown arms
To hold him fast.

"Don't Go to Gothic"

Sometimes I want to say to travelers,
"Don't go to Gothic,
That tender beauty with the emerald fire, who,
By all the old rights of discovery
And of first love,
Too swift and sweet to share,
Belongs to me."

I should not say,
"Don't go to Gothic,
To find a town
Like May Night with a wild rose in her hair,"
For you will go
And never see my claim stakes driven there
And you will not remember
She belongs to me.

Curtain Call

A century and some odd years ago,
The lights dimmed and the curtains rose
And the stage was set with the Rockies for the backdrop.
The spotlight focused on red-bearded Gregory
Who saw four dollars in his frying pan
And shouted, "Gold!"

So the wagons came like ants
And men goaded the oxen
Over the hardpan ruts.

Framed in a wagon bow,
Sometimes a young girl-mother came
With eyes that feared horizons, sear and wide—
With arms that hushed a baby to her breast.

Sometimes a woman walked—
Her basque laced tight to hold her heart in wilderness—
Her skirt full-free to step where stride is great—
Her feet stripped bare to feel the temper of the dust
And save her shoes.

And so they came,
Intending to go back
But staying past their time.

Now Tabor came and splattered silver across the stage
And broke a heart and found one new
And women who had burned their skin in mountain sun,
Shuddered and were half-fearful if their men should find
    the lode.
Some men built castles on the Denver streets
And some were lonely there.

The drama rolled with tragedy and clown.
A whispy-whiskered man urged young men west.
The undertow sucked back bewildered Utes.

Men sought a vein in the Mount Pisgah scene
But made their graveyard there and buried hopes.
A gray-haired carpenter dreamed of a golden strike
And was transformed to Midas overnight.

This was the tide that could not be held back
As men carved names on granite canyon walls
While some were trampled under hobnailed boots.
This was the scene where all the leads and bit-parts
Fit snug as blueprints for refining mill.

Some knew this country in a gentler mood.
To them she gave no fortune but herself.

Sometimes strange figures haunt old trails at dusk
To stalk the sun whose path leads always west.
As though across a western prairie stage,
Old ghosts line up for curtain call—
Young Gregory, still dazed by color in the pan,
Stratton bewildered by the constant weight of gold—
Womack dogged to his death by Fortune's hand.

Faint as through a tear-mist gauze,
A young girl-mother, framed in a wagon bow,
Rides with Future at her breast.

The Silver Ghost of Fryer Hill

A silvered wraith sometimes appears on moonlight nights
And bars a cabin door upon the world
As she was wont to do in life.
Then, wrapping spirit veil about her ghostly head,
Slips like the mist upon a frosted hill
To check the Matchless and to know it safe.

The Matchless is as ghostly now as she
Who haunts it.
She whom the world judged faithless
Has not proved so.
There are promises to keep
Even past death.

The Matchless checked,
Its treasure found untouched,
She winds the fog-like shawl about her shivering form
And fades into the night.

Note: When Silver King Horace Tabor threw over his wife, Augusta, to marry 28-year-old Elizabeth "Baby" Doe, the nation was scandalized. Horace lost his fortune, but on his deathbed, he elicited a promise from Baby Doe that she would never sell the Matchless Mine. Baby Doe lived in poverty at the mouth of the mine on Fryer Hill in Leadville, for the remaining 35 years of her life.

Stone Cutter

I came from Italy to work
In Marble Town one day
And all because with sculpture tools
I had a certain way.

I took a pride in being best.
I put the rest to shame.
I carved the stones for mansions.
I made myself a name.

I worked on many a masterpiece.
But it cut me to the bone
To carve a little curly lamp
Upon my baby's stone.

Of Burros and Men

For Prunes, the Burro at Fairplay

We said he was an ornery critter
Stubborn and hell-mean at times.
We cursed him, beat him on his tough old hide
With lash and bolt
And hobbled him at night to graze.
Then when the deep snow closed the trail
We put him out upon the town to beg.

But when he died, we built a monument
The way folks make up for the things
They didn't do, or say, or remember.
We built it out of granite,
Like the rock that wore his hooves
Down to the quick.

Here we remembered toil and sweat
And a brute sort of fidelity
And our own asininity at times.

Here we remembered that whether we plod or race
When the trail is closed
We all stand
Beggars before God.

Ruin at Romely

The sunlight is quiet now,
Lacing itself with shadow
And stretching its warm shape
Upon the ground.

An old house lies sprawled by fire and storm
And rocks have rolled to stone her
Like a fallen woman,
Once betrayed and past the needing.

Here and there an assay furnace
Stands, outwitting time,
While crucibles, cracked and begrimed
Stare with empty sockets into sun.

There in a cleft of rock,
The frost and rime and columbine
Have split with no less certainty than atom power.

Where once the fury of the strike
Out roared the wind,
The scene is quiet
And the tall pines hush
The grieving of the stream.

Rough Etching

They said, "She used to be a madam—
Ran a house across the creek
But hopes folks have forgotten."
But though the Lord made ten commandments,
None is so scarlet and indelible as one.

I looked at her aging face
Tried to read the wrinkles.
Far as I could see, the lines
Were only drawn by Time and told me nothing.

I noted she was growing deaf
And her voice echoed like a room
Where everything has been removed.

I wondered if she did a penance for remembered sin
Or did she cling to triumph when her hat held plumes
And when her dress laughed with the swish of taffeta
And garters glistened.
They said she cried a great deal now
But her tears seemed meaningless—not repentant—
Just a kind of weakness that comes with years.
And her laughter echoed down a dark forgotten corridor.

School House, Abandoned

My camera registers the ruin of today
With textbooks torn and scattered—
Rusted stove with ashes in the pan
And wood bin emptied long ago and not refilled,
And the shelf without the dipper
Or the pail.

The old platform is smaller now
Than when we all were Patrick Henry
On a Friday afternoon.

I walk instinctively to find a certain desk.
With eyes half closed,
I run my hungry fingers on the dusty top
To find a carved and lettered heart,
Cut by a Christmas knife
To last "so long as grasses grow and rivers run—"

There is a rat-gnawed rope.
I wonder what would happen
And what ghosts would wake
If I should ring the bell?

Ellie Mae

The night is clear and the wind is still
And I hear a cry on Heartbreak Hill.

And I recall in my memory
Just such a night and a girl and me.

The wind was sharp and the leaves turned brown
The night I rode to Cattle Town.

Saturday night and the Bar Magrue
Rocked with gin and a Square Dance too.

I was new in town and I thought I'd glance
At who was swingin' in the dance.

So I shuffled in to the fiddler's time
To find a dancin' gal for mine.

When suddenly I turned to see
A gal a smilin' up at me.

She was pink and white and gold haired too
So what was a guy like me to do?

For she fit right into my good right arm
And I fell a victim to her charm.

A locket hung from her throat so fair
And a rose smelled sweet in her golden hair.

Oh, we do-si-doed and Texas Starred
And that gal caught me off my guard.

And then the caller called out this,
"Round that couple and steal a kiss!"

So I fell in love while we danced the night
But it wasn't meant to turn out right.

As I good-night waltzed her past the door
She slipped away to return no more.

And the night grew calm and the night grew still
And a coyote wailed on Heartbreak Hill.

Oh, I've asked all over the valley side
Where they thought a girl like this might hide.

And some folks laughed and they thought me queer
And said I was drunk on gin and beer.

But one old timer told me then
A tale forgotten by most men.

The story was of Ellie Mae
Who came to Cattle Town, one day.

And her step was light and her face was fair
And she wore a red rose in her hair.

And she fell in love with a certain lad
A handsome buck by the name of Chad.

But a dance hall gal named Mollie Dee
Shot her dead from jealousy.

And they carried her so white and still
To the graveyard up on Heartbreak Hill.

But it's lonely there for Ellie Mae
When the dancers swing and the dancers sway.

And sometimes when the leaves turn brown
Ellie Mae comes back to town.

And sometimes when the wind is still
You can hear her cry on Heartbreak Hill.

It's many years since I came to town
And I should have left, but I've hung around.

And I still go back to the old dance floor
To look for her but she comes no more.

And the fiddlers play and sometimes I sing
And I search each face as I weave that ring.

And they say I'm queer and perhaps it's true
But I do what it seems that I have to do.

And I drink too much as an old man will
And I wander up on Heartbreak Hill.

And the past grows dim and the old dreams go
How much is real I do not know.

But I always keep in my inside pocket
A faded rose and a tarnished locket.

And I hold them tight and my heart stands still
When I hear a cry on Heartbreak Hill.

At Redstone

Idealists have always been the losers
After their fashion,
Leaving heartache for inheritance
And ashes to a grieving wind.
Yet, every loser once faces the grave choice—
Temptation on the mountain—
Barter for the kingdoms of the world—
Protection for the foot against the stone,
And chooses his crucifixion
To know one moment of high ecstasy
Worth all.

Idealists will always be the losers
To all the Shavian Undershafts—
To the munition makers
And to the Caesars of their time.

So it was when Osgood was in Redstone,
When mercy flowered crimson for a day
And then passed into memory
With ashes in the wind.

Note: John C. Osgood was the great humanitarian industrialist who fought for the control of the Colorado Fuel and Iron Company—and lost.

Chipeta at Montrose

It was the rocking chair she hated.
Most white men's complexes she took
With certain reservations.

She could conform to Monday, wash and Tuesday iron,
The red flowers on the carpet
Were pretty when the snow came down.
But the rocking chair she gave wide berth—
That demon that could reach out in the dark
To crack the shins.

The buggy was all right,
Though not like riding bare-back in the wind.
The stove was bad,
An iron devil hotter than the white man's hell!

It was the rocking chair she hated,
Making her seasick; she was alien to the sea!
It was the rocking chair
Where white mothers rocked their babies.
It was the rocking chair
Reminding of her hungry arms
That held no papoose of her own.

Note: Chipeta, Queen of the Utes, lived 1843 - 1924. She and Chief Ouray were childless.

The Galloping Goose at Old Telluride

It is hard to believe, though perhaps it is best
That the Galloping Goose has come to rest.

In old Telluride where once she could fly,
Halfway between the earth and the sky.

She would jump the tracks and the rails would break
And the people get out and rub their ache.

And her riders would help repair the rail
Or whatever caused the Goose to fail.

Then back to their seats to count up to ten
And the Goose would gallop along again.

She looks so peaceful resting there
With never a bump and never a care.

But does she feel a sad regret
And does she sit or does she set,

Hatching the mischief she knows so well—
Her own particular brand of hell?

Or does she mourn her sorry plight
And buck and gallop after night

Past Ophir's gold and Lizard Head,
Or is the Galloping Goose quite dead?

Note: The Galloping Goose was a hybrid means of transportation on the old Ophir Loop on the Rio Grande Southern. It carried seven passengers and freight. Part Pierce Arrow and part train, it ran on tracks and no one ever forgot a ride on the "Goose."

Keepers of the Sheep

The bighorns come down the Tarryall
Each year to mate and winter
And to rear the lambs
Until the ice breaks and the high ridge
Calls them back.

These were our sheep
To coax with red salt and to guard
With fence and gun and threatening oath.
All through the frost November
We could hear the pistol crack of horns
When two rams fought.
"Using the head in love," we said,
"Brings headaches, but it settles things."

Even the shutter bugs we came to fight
Because they spooked the herd
And chased them into photogenic spots.

Most of all we hated the curator
Armed with paper giving him the right
To one fine ram—the best of course,
To stand magnificently stuffed and stilled
Before uncaring hordes
Who never ventured off the pavement.

Lung worm took some. And some were trapped
And carted off to tourist traps. A few hid out
In higher land to stave off civilization and its bars.

A few still come, remembering red salt,
And the half protection of barbed wire and posted fence
And profane ranchers who would hold a futile line
Against encroaching tides.

Scarlet Thread

There are just two kinds of women
And she was that kind—
Too generous and careless with her heart
And bound to end up bankrupt.

If she could trace her ancestry to the Mayflower,
She didn't try—out of respect to the ancestor.
Yet, she had a bond of sympathy with outcast Eve,
The mother of us all.
And she could point to her profession as the oldest
Though not with pride.

Not always, but sometimes, in the early evening
When the houseboy lit the lamps
And a red ray fell across her narrow crib,
She thought of Rahab and the scarlet thread.

Loss

I tried to sleep…went early to bed
"This thing happens to others…" I said.
But two o'clock…the world turns over in its sleep.'
And I lie staring dry eyed…I can't weep.
I will get up and light the light once more.
Maybe it was a dream…I've dreamed such dreams before.
It was no dream. The telegram's there yet.
And it still reads, "We regret."
September 8th, it says…I can't remember well.
What happened then? Would an old paper tell?
There is a stack of papers that I tied
Maybe I could find it if I tried
Ah, here it is … not much … my heart will bleed.
My hands shake so … Do I dare read?
"STRATEGIC POINTS WERE TAKEN IN THE FIGHT."
A little more … It says, "THE LOSS WAS SLIGHT."

The night's black dark envelops all the earth.
The world is shrouded in funereal dearth.
The laughter in the wind forever gone.
I should be brave, but I had only one.
Tonight my heart may break and I may cry
Before the dawn lights up the eastern sky.
But with the day I must be brave again,
Brave as becomes the mothers of such men.
My rosary, I'll tell with fingers numb.
My heart may weep, but quivering lips be dumb.
Surely I read it … but it can't be right
Still, here it is… It says, "THE LOSS WAS SLIGHT!"

Old Construction Worker at the Circle Bar

Why does that old man cash his checks at the Circle Bar
And leave the half of it for drinks and gambling?
Does he not know that money which he makes
Should be spent sparingly and budgeted
And saved for leaner days?
This job won't last forever—he should save!
And well he knows—but all day he has worked down
"In the hole," with dust and sun and wind
Parching his throat and water will not quench
The thirst and hunger that is there—a hunger for far more
Than water or for food or gambling or for women!
It is a strange unrest ... a gnawing ... or a seeking ...
Maybe after God, Himself! Who knows?

Somewhere within the gin-cloud of his memory, he gazes back
To days when he was young and hoped for much.
He did not dream that he could be an old man
Broken down and muckin' on a dam!
When he was young, he dreamed his dreams.
Somewhere along the way, he missed the turn.
Gin helps forget the failure ... wife at home ... everything
Until Monday when you get back on the dam again.

Shakily he thrusts a gnarled hand into his muddy jeans
And brings it out filled with small shiny coins.
He'll play the slot machine once more although he knows
Even if he hits the jackpot, it will all go back again.
Ten cent offerings to the God of Chance
From one who lost his luck!

Ticket to Silverton

The ticket specifies "Today—to Silverton,"
But I shall scan
A rhythmic sonnet of small wheels
That beat out accent on the jointed rails
To catch a yester song.

I will set Time back
To breathe the coal oil in the unlit lamps—
To feel warmth in the old pot-bellied stove—
To see men, once unafraid of height or depth—
Remember women whose pale skin belied
A tensile strength akin to corset steel.
And I will set Time up
To reach to future skies, swift scribed by wings
That may forget these little trains.

I will come back to the coach
With some whose fancy always measures "narrow gauge"—
Whose boundaries are certain designated seats—
Who stray no farther than the "Ladies' Room."

These narrow rails go fifty miles or so
But I shall go much farther than the tickets show.

Ranch Story

The children wanted to stay home with me tonight,
But I said, "No. I want this night alone."
I'm not afraid. A ranch wife seldom is.

I did not cry—not even when adobe clods fell on his box
Like heavy periods to mark the end and seal the day forever.
Death could not prime dry eyes that spent their tears on life.

This is the place John brought me as a bride.
Those are the windows opening wide
To boundaries enlarged with every year,
And there—the new barn that we built to hold our gains.

This is the room where I came as a girl and then as wife
And where my babies first found breath
And where he died.

He meant well. But times were hard and help was scarce,
So side by side, he and the horses and I pulled to make
    things go.
Oh, I was strong and even when the babies came, I worked
And he forgot I was a woman with small needs
And I forgot it, too.
There was that summer late in life—the one when Ted was born,
And Jim, my oldest, summer-schooling to get through
And John, resenting his not harvesting the crop,
And so I drove the team all summer in the field
And I was brown and burned by sun and big with Ted.

That was the time the teacher came to live
And she was pale and gold and like a willow
　　in a light blue rain,
Or like a warm Chinook that sets the brook to surging in
　　the spring.

It was my pride that hurt, and not my heart that broke,
For I was past that first wild need that flamed
　　and begged in her.
Old Doc said, "Patience—patience—he'll come
　　back to you"
And Doc was right for Jim came home and took
　　her from his dad!

I do not know if Jimmy loved her
Or if he did it just for me. But it was hard on all.
It hurts to see a strong man humbled by his son.

Tomorrow, Jim will bring her here and they
　　will run the ranch.
A ranch must have a man, I know.
I'll move all my belongings to this room.
Death seals no day
Nor puts an end to memory that will not die.
After tonight, let her come back
And I will watch this ranch break her.

Why I Stay

The West is fickle,
Freezing or burning with a breath.
She has no consistency.
Once when the sun caught fire
Upon an aspen hill,
She made false promises of gold to me,
But long ago had given to another one
Who found her first.
The rarest thing she ever put into my hand
Was a mariposa
With a hummingbird throat.

The only reason that I stay
Is that I love her.